AWESOME DOGS

Pomeranians

by Domini Brown

BELLWETHER MEDIA • MINNEAPOLIS, MN

Note to Librarians, Teachers, and Parents:

Blastoff! Readers are carefully developed by literacy experts and combine standards-based content with developmentally appropriate text.

Level 1 provides the most support through repetition of high-frequency words, light text, predictable sentence patterns, and strong visual support.

Level 2 offers early readers a bit more challenge through varied simple sentences, increased text load, and less repetition of high-frequency words.

Level 3 advances early-fluent readers toward fluency through increased text and concept load, less reliance on visuals, longer sentences, and more literary language.

Level 4 builds reading stamina by providing more text per page, increased use of punctuation, greater variation in sentence patterns, and increasingly challenging vocabulary.

Level 5 encourages children to move from "learning to read" to "reading to learn" by providing even more text, varied writing styles, and less familiar topics.

Whichever book is right for your reader, Blastoff! Readers are the perfect books to build confidence and encourage a love of reading that will last a lifetime!

This edition first published in 2017 by Bellwether Media, Inc.

No part of this publication may be reproduced in whole or in part without written permission of the publisher. For information regarding permission, write to Bellwether Media, Inc., Attention: Permissions Department, 5357 Penn Avenue South, Minneapolis, MN 55419.

Library of Congress Cataloging-in-Publication Data

Names: Brown, Domini, author.
Title: Pomeranians / by Domini Brown.
Other titles: Blastoff! Readers. 2, Awesome Dogs.
Description: Minneapolis, MN : Bellwether Media, Inc., [2017] | Series:
   Blastoff! Readers. Awesome Dogs | Audience: Ages 5-8. | Audience: K to
   grade 3. | Includes bibliographical references and index.
Identifiers: LCCN 2015048420 | ISBN 9781626173941 (hardcover : alk. paper)
Subjects: LCSH: Pomeranian dog–Juvenile literature. | Toy dogs–Juvenile
   literature. | Dog breeds–Juvenile literature.
Classification: LCC SF429.P8 B76 2017 | DDC 636.76–dc23
LC record available at http://lccn.loc.gov/2015048420t

Printed in the United States of America, North Mankato, MN.

Table of Contents

What Are Pomeranians?

Pomeranians are lively dogs. They are called Poms for short.

Though small, this **breed** has big character!

Pomeranians have thick, soft fur.
Owners must brush them often.

A full **undercoat** keeps Poms warm. Their outer fur is long and straight.

Poms come in more than 18 **coat** colors. Many are orange, black, or cream.

Pomeranian Coats

merle   parti-color

Some Poms have patterned coats. They can be **merle** or **parti-color**.

Big **ruffs** of fur surround their necks. The ruffs sometimes hide their small, triangle-shaped ears.

Long, fluffy tails curl up on Poms' backs.

History of Pomeranians

Pomeranians came from larger **spitz** dogs.

Small Poms began in Pomerania. This is now Germany and Poland. There, people **bred** Poms down in size.

The smaller dogs made good **companions**.

In the late 1800s, Queen Victoria of England owned Poms. She helped the breed become popular.

Today, Poms are favorite pets
for their size and spirit.

Pomeranian Profile

small body

triangle-shaped ears

fluffy tail

Life Span: 14 to 16 years

Trainability:

| 1 | 2 | 3 | 4 | 5 | 6 |

Hardest to train   Easiest to train

The dogs are in the **Toy Group** of the **American Kennel Club**.

Spirited Companions

Pomeranians are high spirited. They easily learn new tricks and commands.

Many Poms like to have jobs. Some comfort people as **therapy dogs**.

Sometimes Poms are loud. They bark when they sense danger or get excited.

Their small size does not stop them from having fun!

Glossary

American Kennel Club—an organization that keeps track of dog breeds in the United States

bred—purposely mated two dogs to make puppies with certain qualities

breed—a type of dog

coat—the hair or fur covering an animal

companions—friends who keep someone company

merle—a pattern that is one solid color with patches and spots of another color

parti-color—a pattern that is mainly one color, but with patches of one or more other colors

ruffs—areas of longer fur around the necks of some animals

spitz—a group of dog breeds with heavy coats and curled tails that are from cold areas of the world

therapy dogs—dogs that comfort people who are sick, hurt, or have a disability

Toy Group—a group of the smallest dog breeds; most dogs in the Toy Group were bred to be companions.

undercoat—a layer of short, soft hair or fur that keeps some dog breeds warm

To Learn More

AT THE LIBRARY

Landau, Elaine. *Pomeranians Are the Best!*
Minneapolis, Minn.: Lerner, 2011.

Lee, J. H. *Boo: The Life of the World's Cutest Dog.*
San Francisco, Calif.: Chronicle Books, 2011.

Mattern, Joanne. *Pomeranians.* Edina, Minn.: ABDO
Pub. Company, 2012.

ON THE WEB
Learning more about
Pomeranians is as easy
as 1, 2, 3.

1. Go to www.factsurfer.com.

2. Enter "Pomeranians" into the search box.

3. Click the "Surf" button and you will see a
   list of related web sites.

With factsurfer.com, finding more
information is just a click away.

Index